Praise for Kevin Miller

Home & Away: The Old Town Poems

In *Home and Away: The Old Town Poems*, nearly every poem has the home court advantage. When Kevin Miller writes about place, for example, each locale becomes local: just around the corner, in the classroom, at the supper table or behind the fruit stand up the road. The poems in this remarkable book are often wry, wistful and yet also hopeful. These pages offer the glitz of going out, the peace of coming home.
>　　　—Allen Braden, *A Wreath of Down and Drops of Blood*

There's a lush, visceral domesticity to these poems, even as they travel to other places, peoples, and times. 'Days are made of small acts,' Miller writes, and here are the acts evoked compellingly, in some cases hauntingly, and revealed as the biggest things we know. These are not safe poems. They are placed and peopled like a Raymond Carver story or an Edward Hopper painting. The poet's own vulnerabilities share the pages with the 'homes and aways' of others, of friend, family, and stranger. This is a sharply empathetic poet whose poems, as they reveal the extraordinary in the everyday, serve to deepen our time together.
>　　　—Derek Sheffield, *Through Second Skin*

Everywhere Was Far

These poems don't stand still. No one, and no place, can claim them. There is water everywhere. Spokane. Drumgildra. Grenaa. Navarra Coulee. Arletta. So much of the water is river. These are Kevin Miller's poems. They are close enough to remember, far enough to keep running up there, past here, to somewhere else. All along the way, steady.
>　　　—Barry Grimes, *This Green*

VANISH

VANISH

Kevin Miller

Wandering Aengus Press
Eastsound, WA

Library of Congress Cataloguing-in-Publication Data available.

First Edition

Winner of the 2019 Wandering Aengus Press Award

Poetry
ISBN: 978-0-578-63213-1

Cover Image: "Ghost Trees" by Vance Thompson

Author Photo: Cameon Miller

Wandering Aengus Press is dedicated to publishing works to
enrich lives and make the world a better place.

Wandering Aengus Press
PO Box 334 Eastsound, WA 98245
wanderingaenguspress.com

What falls away is always. And is near.
                              —Theodore Roethke

—*for Seamus, Liam, Finnian, Maeve, Colm, & Sullivan*

Contents

VANISH

Acknowledgments

The author would like to thank the following publications in which these poems or forms of these poems have previously appeared.

Apple Valley Review: "When You Finish," "New Roses, Neuralgia"

Barely South Review: "Field Work"

Being: What Makes a Man: "Chrome and Oranges"

Cirque: "What You Refused to Tell"

Clover: "Becoming Piaget's Car"

Crab Creek Review: "Pull Dates," "Last Night Your Mother," "It's Like Feeding Horses," "Luck," "Painting: *Bandana in Barn Window*," "Smoke & Miracles," "Pen and Ink of Mother"

damfino: "She Lifts the Song"

Floating Bridge 7: "Orphan Winter Find Us"

Massachusetts Review: "Chrome and Oranges"

Museum of Americana: "Dink's Tune"

Poetry 129, Washington State anthology: "About George"

Pontoon: "A Box of Rocks"

Raven Chronicles: "On Jane's Table Everything's for Sale," "Yard Work"

San Pedro River Review: "What's Eating Her?" "Jack and the Wagon," "What Is Left"

Spitball: "Hike with My Father in Mind"

Spry Literary Journal: "Casey Drops Blue"

Switched on Gutenberg: "In Johanna's Corner"

Terrain.Org: "Letter to America" "Swan Song," "Smoke & Miracles: Four Parts," "For Iben, Almost Forty," "Gray with an *A*," "Oh Brother"

The Burnside Review "The Bureau of Wear and Tear"

The Nassau Review: "Finishing the Chores"

The Oregonian: "Vanish"

Windfall: "Early Winter, Old Town"

Wrist Mag: "Missing Jim Crabtree"

I am grateful to the following for support and help with this project: Derek Sheffield, Casey Fuller, Vance Thompson, Jim Bodeen, Barry Grimes, Jill McCabe Johnson, Tina Schumann, Nance Van Winckel, Paula Meehan, Nancy Takacs.

A grant from the Tacoma Artists Initiative Program and the Tacoma Arts Commission supported this work.

Vanish

whispers its swish of sound
as a trail of breath follows
an image you hold like the title
of the film you saw two nights
ago, no longer on the tip of anything,
no aftertaste, no crumbs to help
find your way back to a place
you forget being, this little tremor
of fear when the ripples left
by the stone fail to reach the edge,
and the pond is a space as dark
as swallows you remember returning
to the nook above the door
in the garage behind the house
you find only in your sleep.

White Shirts

Chrome and Oranges

Some days I drag what I have done
like a sack of wet laundry,

the more I lug the heavier it gets,
and if I don't tend to it, it sours.

Tub of guts, we said as kids—
it had nothing to do with towing,

still this knowing attracts flies.
Might as well add envy to the pile,

jealous as I am of those able to forget.
And while stench may be a trigger,

I cannot recall the name of the woman
at work who smelled like shower steam

on powdered skin every morning for ten
glorious years. Instead, something I said

to J.B. forty years ago appears like a bull
on the highway. It gives asphalt a lesson

on black, leaves me replaying a stupid beef
over a woman who left both of us.

The Christmas I was ten I rode my new bike
to Richard's to show off all that chrome.

He showed me checkers and an orange.
Those handlebars rust at the bottom of the sack.

Bad days, I hang each item on a line.
They sag like wet squares of sheetrock.

From a distance, you might wonder how
one man could own so many white shirts.

Pull Dates

The cottage cheese, yogurt,
and milk promise life,
their impressed guarantee assures
a fast forward to vacation,
weeks of possibility, and drives
a stake in accident's heart.

On a good day the grocery cart works.
The list says salsa, salmon, mousetraps,
and foil—it lines a path away from death
though worry queries if it should read
mice, if there are lemons at home,
if counting chickens hatches
a sinister confidence in longevity
and calls for a pinch of salt
over the shoulder of positive thoughts.

A man alone shopping has considerations,
six pack or twelve, salted or unsalted butter,
decaf or regular, two percent or blue water—
each hesitation a fear-stuffed Oreo.
If his numbers were posted, he might
head directly for chips and a cheesecake
to follow the marbled beef.

If someone had written *not much longer*
on the tail of his laundered shirt,
he'd grant clemency to the mice,
buy a pack of Luckies,
and when the machine asked *cash back?*
he'd punch *all of it*
take everyone out to dinner.

Becoming Piaget's Car

Playing with the toddler, you push
the toy car under the chair, and
there is no car. You know this truth,
driven as you have been to be seen.
It's quiet under the chair, darker
though more like sleep than clouds.
Ideas like chrome and horn vanish.
Idling is as automatic as breath, still
you remember the way in and imagine
an other side, though lately you worry
if no one expects to see you, you might
have crossed over rather than under.

New Roses, Neuralgia

Something in the nerve endings burns
deep as if the bone core were hot wire,
the charley horse pales, this,
this is all the yellow jackets at once
sawing between marrow and skin,
you pace, sit, pace, the kneading tricks
fail, and you feel the fool for wincing,
your dead father says Walk it off,
walk it off, self-pity is a garish shirt
all rhinestones and me, so you pound
on the calf, beat one mark to blot
out another, the unreachable hurt
fades as the self-made surfaces
and you wish back yesterday's soft rain
as thin as sloughed skin, you long
to wear it like a shawl and you think
you remember your mother buttering
your burned hand, you know she stops
a bleeding knee with gauze and tape,
and later, the fever, blood poisoning's
red stripe up your leg, she puts you
in a cab with no way to pay doctor
or hack, she smiles like Lauren Bacall,
as if beauty and prayer are collateral,
she waves, exhales a zephyr
of Chesterfield smoke, deftly picks
tobacco from her tongue, and slowly
disappears like this ache and the idea of it.

The Bureau of Wear and Tear

This drawer holds enough black socks
for twenty funerals, and while I prefer
to wear them to weddings, odds are poor
at my age. Since I gave up the tie job,
they lie like blocks of turf gone flat
before fire, and since the nieces, nephews,
and former students have all married,
the last five occasions have been parents
of friends, and friends. The nearest grand
kid wedding has to be about fifteen years
away, and while I have saved one pair
for my youngest brother who has waited
half a century to ring the bells, the rest
wait like toe tags. Sometimes I open
this drawer and feel like I am the cause.
Like black crossed bones they rattle
their way into the world.
Superstition rides with me each day:
I use the same cup for coffee,
turn this light off last before leaving,
always lock the bottom lock first.
You might think habit, fine, habit it is,
habits broken have consequences
I refuse to name for naming gives them life.
This line at the post office, this checker
at the grocery, that lane one mile from work—
this is the physical ritual of prayer where
faith is a missing person with no photo.
Yes, though I wander from talk of socks,
I have a plan, this pair for my brother
I will keep for other nuptials if they occur,
the rest I will burn after each ceremony
of the dark suit, and when fires consume
the final pair, I will be barefoot and ready
to be laid out on a table others will circle
with whiskey and stout as black as hose.

Recidivism: Opening Day

Burned oatmeal smokes
on the back porch,
the open window starts
a cloud exchange.
The kitchen fan goes nowhere,
this healthy breakfast smudges a day
bacon might have cured.
Someone said worry is a form of prayer,
a devotion lost on pharmacists.
Pending indulgences digest best
sans thought, say cheese, say please
pass the hash-browns. My father dieted
to a potassium-deficiency-heart-attack—
Jack be nimble, Jack be quick,
Jack would be here if he settled for thick.
My fingers recall the smooth feel
of a Lucky Strike as I spin a pint glass,
my right hand cracks the safe.
I utter my last healthy words.

Your Name on the Board

The cursive leans into wind
as if a breeze cushions the slant.
Sister writes your letters board-left,
and you relish the way it starts
with her swirling capital *K*,
the one you practice and use

for years without attribution.
To ensure longevity, you earn two
checks, negative attention has legs,
and you want to practice all five
letters before they disappear.
Infamy trumps compliance,
see Dick and Jane run amok.

Your foray lasts until the note
home, her method pure Palmer
streams like spun glass, chronicles
sins venial until your father deems
them mortal, this one-man Legion
of Decency whose own hand-cut
strong, elegant letters you keep
bound and safe in your desk drawer.

Yard Work

You love the scuffle hoe,
extend, pull, and scrape
the surface a thin skim
as if removing the moles
on your spotted skin or
peeling a layer of years
from the face of it all,
leather and weather,
crow's feet and furrow,
tags and other bits.
Or this spring you use
the handle as support.
You see the way weeds
cover the bed you made,
the lie in it others want
you to see, straight edges
and borders, the order they
love. You want a smoke,
the ease of exhaling
while you ponder. Each
season you rework skin
to callous, the other side
of liver spots, you joke
about connecting dots,
the constellation of scars
for stars, a map to trace
labor days, buck twenty-
five an hour, ten-cent beers
and fears this was your life.

Hike with My Father in Mind
Mt. Rainier, Washington

My father hated the Boy Scouts.
Something to do with men and
boys in the same tent, distrust
of anyone who refused sports.
I learned to block the curve ball
in the dirt, take it off my chest
and keep it ready to play.
Building a fire in any weather
was beyond my practice.
No man in the woods is saved
by his ability to handle the short
hop, framing a pitch does little
for one's sense of direction.
My experience with bears was
the Yakima Bears, the only stars
I can name are The Mick, Roger,
and Yogi. I was taught to revere
constellations like Satchel and Jackie.
No hiker ever found his way to safety
following Van Lingo Mungo
in the night sky. Still, I persist
on the trail to Spray Park, the bugs
and dust nothing when you know
how to take one for the team.

This Land Is Your Land

Never give a drunk a gun, instead,
let's corral as many drunks as we can
next to the banks of any body of water—
ocean, bay, river, reservoir, plastic bottle,
inflatable pool without children.
Let's give them fire and short fuses, red
white and blue T-shirts arcing over boilers
built with pilsner and fast food, tell them
this is their country and they must make
a party of gun powder and pressed paper.
When they wake to their hangovers and
mustard stains, everyone else is a lost dog.

Gray with an *A*

Unpicked apples last the winter,
hangings and other ornamentals.
Leaves are a turn ahead, February
appears too soon for all this wool,
for those waiting to finish the two-
winter novel all war and no peace
except hummingbirds and bushtits
firing like the only ideas in this fog
and trapped smoke. Excuses say

exactly what you want to hear,
trust yourself to buffer the stillness,
lost faith makes a small mark, stays.
A dog outside a barbershop follows
you home, this itch under the collar.
You miss a good storm, real dark
begs tomato soup and toasted cheese
sandwiches, everything your mother
believed requires a cumulonimbus sky.

What You Refused to Tell

The wrecked affair, screen door
slams wood-clap and rattle,
the latch-hook swings its best

pendulum imitation, winds down
after all the commotion quick exits
bring, and the quiet after, cigarette

smoke rises in the beautiful folds
ribbons love, what was undone hung
like the death of a cheap toaster.

Caution tape and lights masquerade
as crime regalia. To cross this line
requires paper slippers and gloves.

The chalk outlines a story, he's missing—
not some dime-store ghost, his end lasts
beyond the credits, white letters on glass,

your mother on the lip of a chair leans
into the room, hands in her lap,
a Chesterfield between fingers, another

in the ashtray. When she sees you
in the hall, she waves away smoke,
points to you and says, *Not now. Not now.*

Swan Song

—after Tyge Ingerslev's *Kolindsund 2011*

Watercolor is a controlled bleed,
its edges feathered in airy layers,
brush, paint, paper, and the complex
mastery of water.

Gradations of gray frame
swan ghosts gliding twice white,
each a note composed as the train
crosses flat land to Århus Station,

winter 1990, Kolind is all pond
glass out the window the smooth
idle a mute ease trumpeting water's
return, reclaiming reclaimed fields.

Today the disappeared lake's
striations line like sheet music
pressed on a schoolhouse shade
drawn past return, what's dun

was water pumped and drained,
what's left is bottomland too wet
to farm, rushes at the deckle edge
recall the refrain of lake, of swan.

The Paper Heart

Turn of the Heart

She says the woolly worm's stripes
foretell dark days, this brown stripe
is a line crossed at your own risk,
enjoy this light, for it will disappear
like good days after bad. I cut, split,
and stack on the outside chance
we make it to winter. This spring
metamorphoses from one black
stripe to another, the Isabella tiger
moth gives way to another mother,
say bald-faced hornet, say yellow jacket,
the whirring turn of the paper heart,
stinger and stung swell together,
this wife's tale promises a sharp end.

Woman with Candle

Because she bows, because she faces
the candle and lilacs out the window,
you will not see the green of her eye
nor the parts flecked hazel. Notice
her hands, their delicate bone as fine
as a scrimshander's line, consider
their stillness. Wait for the rise and fall
of the body breathing, let it draw you
into its rhythm, each breath, the room,
you, the woman centered at the flame
and its reflection. The light now, and then.

Last Call

At her desk she keeps a bowl of spent matches.
The ceremony of smoke and light is breath too.

What she started in spring arrives late, its nub
as firm as a knuckle touching the pane.

November stills sepal and a slip of petal
rapt in the last dance at closing time.

The morning after wind and rosebuds wake her,
she weaves the cane of a late-blooming rose

into the curved metal staff holding
the hummingbird feeder, the sugar water

a blossom of red to coddle those staying
for winter. I missed the single touch to glass

she imagined, missed her deep breaths
to wash clean the last thoughts of day.

What We Miss

Hatred consumes the news,
what we pass off as hope
appears to be whiskey
in the baby's bottle.
I return to 1990, Grenå's
cobbled walking streets
on a shopping Saturday.
Lines at the post office
buzz with people waiting
to pay for phone and power.
frimærke, frimærke, frimærke
I practice the word for stamp
with *til USA* to follow,
the part I have down.

In town, the rush of fresh-
ground coffee greets me
before the cheese wagon,
each works the offshore breeze.
Our kids are kids missing all day.
We have a list, backpacks, and hours
to listen to locals in the midst
of their lives, to love our place
away, to find joy in the simple
wedge of Klemensker, a cheap
red or white we will carry home
for our one obligation to sit
on the banks of the å to play
What do you miss?

Near Skagen

she rolls her cuffs, drops shoes and socks
puts one foot in the Kattegat, the other
the North Sea. This is the place of light.
Norway one hundred miles northwest
is an idea strong enough to turn clouds.
Sweden, another cousin close enough
for stones, lies forty-three miles east.

Farewell makes such sense by itself,
it's only when followed with a name
or a place it settles like lead in the gut.
This may be her last chance.
Hours later in Anna Ancher's House
she breaks museum rules, photographs
the window in the scullery,
this place where the maid stood
in the painting "Pigen i køkkenet,"
sun northeast to Grenen and the seas.

Everything becomes a last chance,
she swims between *firemen* bobbing
like blazing jelly near Old Skagen,
she tries the fishmonger's smoked mackerel,
she speaks the word for eel—*ål,*
he smiles like she is home.

The Local Patch

At the kitchen counter
we mix hawk and falcon
call them city hawks—
merlin, kestrel, sharp-
shinned and Cooper's.

One tail's not another,
these feeders an hors d'
oeuvres tray set, say
sparrow, towhee, finch.
We jumble key markings,

correct and amend our
coffee birding, bushtits
merit a nod for their bits
of miss safe in suet cages.
Today's finest line is spider

silk spun with lichen, moss,
and leaves, nests able to ex-
pand with hummingbird chicks.
Later a grandson says of his day,
We climbed trees to find sun-

windows. His eyes alive
in the rearview mirror as he
moves an open hand to show
he can push a branch and shade
his eyes to let in the light.

Our world is small, city
blocks for home and away.
What the sky gives we receive,
when the news is a friend's
name, we lean into the clouds.

Early Winter, Old Town

The spurtle lists in the porridge as if the fiber
coalesced and rose to flag this territory for hearts

strong enough for winter. The cold's given itself
to the fog, together they spider like wedding veils

on abandoned lavender, stems of uncut peony,
and humps of heather lining the walk to the
birdbath.

The foghorns drone off Vashon Island, they owe it
to the trains and their arrogant way with time.

The neighbor's fiberglass greenhouse is neither
green
nor house, though it glows in the morning dark

like a church big enough for a small god and you.

Pen and Ink of Mother

Beyond the dammed river,
she carries a basket of apple wood,
wool hat pulled low. She walks
the aisle of sleeping goldens
as if cupped in a tunnel of split ends.
Smoke rises through fog, in first light
the grays form a veiled blessing
over the black line of water.
Clusters of props wedge in the crooks
of trees as if someone finished
preparations for a burning.
Her dogs zigzag the fairway tree
to tree nosing for mice in love
with bark. She finds asparagus
here in spring, secret spots mapped
like clusters of cash she's hidden
in the orchard, though the faces
of her children and their given
names refuse to align. The owl
settles in the packing shed where
she boxed pears, peaches, and cots.
After feeding the coals her basket
of sticks, she will set the kettle,
light a candle at her desk, place
the spent match the same direction
as the others, black ends facing
west where the gold mine swallowed
men who struggled to pay for land.
Before her first cup of tea, she marks
her notebook with the date and time
the light reaches the river.

The Song She Lifts

from the river floats
like tufts of cottonwood
fluff in a tumbling chorus
of hoary-headed elders,
thin boned and delicate
it nicks the surface,
each airy asterisk is a secret.

You hum the water strider's
tune, the hint of willow rises
from the cucumber water
your mother fashions to charm
guests who know half of most
stories and some of others.
The refrain of the lost love

belongs to everyone—those who
listen, those who refuse, what
disappears is a filament so fine
and tangled even the wind tires
of its openings. One end runs
through another and what's not
to love this way the voice stays.

Jack and the Wagon

He's got five years to play, five
years to be a boy who hates clarinet
and loves second base, this the ease
stopping makes before the trouble
adults screw into lives.

A wagon in snow-time
starts the story you know ends
a man alone. A black and white
winter, hat, gloves, mother-love,
a camera—luxuries in 1925.

The wagon's his to load, to fill
with the stories an only child tells
himself, helping his father too drunk
to find the car, a mother left at home
in the odd marriage housewife suggests,

bound to porch, to sink and glass.
Who's siding with whom, four wheels
with only two that turn, he learns
to take sides and the slow burn,
it's tough to hide in ice times,

slammed doors and chores, gone
for good, as if good were a prize
he might win, a boy with no beans
caught in between. Mean casts
its shadow, he scoots his wagon

into the sun and fills it with promises
to his mother to himself, to his six
unimagined children who come late
to the evidence, Jack chose trade,
an empty house the giant he feared.

Orphan Winter Finds Us

sifting photos, your mother
and Clarence in black and white
as if Dorothea Lange found them
at table over Rainier stubbies.
Could we ever be this beautiful,
his white T-shirt, her hair gold
even without color, and the hands,
hers foreshadow your thin fingers,
elegant and hard as polished stone.
His right hand near the beer is thick
scarred from the mines and work
in the orchard the ore bought.

These staked and plotted acres
were his Bing trees till disease
took them both, left us smoke.
Winter was props stacked in trunks,
irrigation sections on the swampers'
flatbed, his all-day apple wood fire,
and the freezer filled with venison.
Even your mother feigned rest
when early snow stilled the valley.
This season, nothing is what it was,
snow's late, hawks work the dry grass,
dogs sleep on the doorsteps waiting
to ride in pickups no one starts.

The End of Grace

Siblings talk recipes, birth order,
lima beans, liver, and other
unknowns. The young ones
knew leathery steak under their
fried onions. Our mother who art
in heaven never baked a pie,
she kept us walking carefully
as angel-food cakes teetered
upside down on the counter.
She made green Jell-O salad
with banana slices suspended,
topped it with mayonnaise
as if color suggested whipped
topping. Under the cover
of darkness she refilled milk
cartons with her dried mix,
and giggled when we gagged
on powder balls. We learned
to be wary of opened containers.
Mother gave stubborn its place
before Irish, served unfinished
dinners at breakfast to sons
who failed to out-wait her.
Our father, also on the other side,
prepared the big dishes, daylong
spaghettis with ribs, chow mein
with soft and hard noodles,
and a rare cracked crab feast—
the only time anyone in our house
wielded a hammer. The family
stigmata—table rules, wears like
inked skin. Hold your fork like this,
elbows off the table, please &
thank you, no short stopping.

Father added I have had sufficient
to every I'm done. Do Not Interrupt,
interrupted interrupters.
We cried over spilt milk. Grace ended,
Amen, Get the goddamned dog
out from under the table.

Oh Brother

These juice glass circles cut
baking powder biscuits, each
opens a disappeared moon
fit to slather in butter, dunk
in white beans with ham
Mom simmers as she folds
the spaces and flattens enough
for the last two wheels she lines
on the cookie sheet, and I fix
dough eyes popped clean
as a brother gone, me in his shirt,
his room mine, out the window
the same laurel hedge he watched
alive with robins' nests, black
branches twisted as thick as a fence
blocking the Paskes' yard, croquet
balls clacking, kids shouting Poison,
rat dog yapping, Old Man Paske,
who never knew me from my brother,
biting his pipe stem, inhaling, launching
a single smoke ring as if he invented air.

When You Finish

tell the one about your uncle who becomes
the empty shirt, tell the part where he pulls
single socks from sleeves as if city hawks
killed all his rabbits, tell how you saw
him when his tricks worked as planned,
when sleight of hand had nothing to do
with shoplifting, before clumsy disguises
trailed him like tasseled quail mocking
his crooked toupee, tell how he sang Sinatra
through cigar smoke the highball ice forever
almost spilling on your aunt's carpet.
Don't forget the part about your wedding,
his toast, tell the kids what he said
about fallen away Catholics and the Jews
in *Ulysses*, then tell what your father said.

Field Work

The five-year-old grandson carries
the short shovel, says, I am a worker.
His hands pulse red in the cold,
and he pounds at the earth
proud to turn soil. He has no notion
of entering the house where brothers
read and play cars. This one will bury me,
his brother will know what to say,
the third will keep mischief alive.
The girl-child from another city
will stand with the boys, her song
long on tradition steeped in rain.
When I threw dirt on my father's box,
spring showers softened the knock
of rocks on its pine door. The windows
in the house of the dead have no glass,
the music their lives make lifts curtains.
The far field knows no distance.

Letter to America

—*after Alison Hawthorne Deming*

Decent people circle close enough
for me to sense their breath,
blood houses align cobbled paths,
we emerge from hedges, snagged
and cut raw, near here water
rushes under bridges, kisses pilings
where banks fail again and again.
For days I return to this word: *decent*.

My grandchildren sigh relieved,
for the *please and thank you* grind
is shelved for a time, they can
snatch, grab, and graze at will.
My *decency* becomes a relief effort,
freedom from the old man's saw,
and while I hunger for an end
to this aberration from the news,

they think, He's wrapped too tight
to object to Pop-Tarts and corn dogs,
he forgets to remind us to put
empty cereal bowls in the sink.
This is a new day, they shake their
heads, giggle, Granddad's gone
on that walk with no direction home.

Cousins under the Japanese Maples

Cherry blossoms spot the garage roof
like first snow—spring breeze sways
the Japanese maples' perfect cover
for children collapsed like toadstools,
who giggle at disappearing in the yard
crowded with adult legs and shoes.
Is it prescient, we fail to see them,
they see us unbending and straight.
Invisible, weightless, the wind will lift
them beyond the fences and fears.
We must keep them safe—every dog,
every car racing nearby becomes a wire
to catch a kite, or branches to tangle
them tails and all, and why not hide
if these boots on the ground mean one
tether after another, mother, father.

Homemade Saints

Consider Brian Wilson's Other Ear

Sunday in late January, everyone shows up in bathrobes,
terrycloth, the ones adding the same ten to fifteen pounds
TV does, so if we film this, everyone is twenty or thirty
ahead while bacon sizzles in the cast-iron pan, tumblers
of OJ ride the counter like orange broncos and the edgy feel
of celebrity gone wrong settles in a room of unknowns.
No one's here to be discovered, footwear makes this clear.
Wing tips and knee socks drop from robes next to Keens,
Converse high-tops, and a daring pair of spiked-heel boots.
Sweet Pea from the bookstore wears an apron over his robe
and wields a spatula like Princess Leia mimicking her
brother.
Today all eggs are scrambled, voices mix in eerie harmony,
dogs bark across the alley. Near the bay, the train to
Portland
whistles as if *Pet Sounds* reached its end as the coffee finishes
with climactic breaths. Guerci shows late wearing a black
robe.
After Opus Dei jokes morph into the supreme injustice
of it all, C makes cinnamon toast, and I raise my Irish coffee
to honor all knees of those in the genuflection drill team.

In Johanna's Corner

Every fighter thinks he's getting up.
Take this whiskey and let it trail
through you, through as you are
with the likes of him.
Wrap your child in this quilt, rock
him slowly and whisper that sound
the doves make huddled from sideways
rain under the bridge at Drumsna.
What we see in your eye closes him
to this place. His people know—
fist unfolds a hand to shade
the shame a son brings home.
Take the scarf from your hair,
let the fiery shock stream from high,
for what they refused to see will burn
its way over the hedgerows and lanes
until he's left alone to cool to stone.

What's Eating Her?

After a trolley ride to Bartell's at Pine Street,
the lunch counter waitress would give us
her smoke and whiskey *Whaddayahave*,
as if we caused her stretch marks.
I had not recalled her piss-off-and-die
for forty-five years until talking this week
with the frail girl in the thin glasses.
Each day she makes my first cup
with grace and a smile as true as clear fir.
She is nothing like the old gruel, still
I sense the black backs of carpenter ants,
the fine dust they make of wood,
their unseen honeycomb winding,
as if the wall would be the last to know.
Her lines are company lines, though I
trust her when she asks of my week,
when she says she can't wait till Sunday
to watch hockey with her brothers.
All week this fear for her gnaws.
Worry is sinister, wind in a hollow world
whispers parts of things, who's to say
what is missed as I hurry through the pleasant.
Would I recognize a morning when her car
wouldn't start, would I sense a twitch
in the eye, catch a hint in her voice
if grief followed her home.

Missing Jim Crabtree

Crab, that sly smile curled
its way across your face
and the stars you had for eyes
glistened like the Waterford
goblets Mother left us, she
and you too, Jimmy, left us
stranded and dumb, muddling
in the kitchen with hand-cut
glassware shelved, and when
the willow leaves have fallen
and a rare winter sun sneaks
its flat line into the kitchen
to bounce off this crystal,
I hold what remains—
the way you said, Hey, Mills,
the mistakes I made, the deep
cut of your death lined in news-
print in a vanished Seattle paper.

Meeting Like This

Jim appears at the bridge
on Yakima Street, I step close

to embrace him. He's a lumpy
little Buddha in an old sweater.

When I open my arms, I'm unsure
what's there is more than air.

All week I wrote, placed him
at Dakota Creek, marked him

with kingfishers and the red line
cutthroat cut close to shore.

No boy fishing the creek,
he appears the grown man, hands

in his pockets, that aw-shucks smile.
His presence feels expected, a secret

agent's live drop, governments
represented without distinction,

men in slept-in clothes fumble
to ford the clumsiness the dead

bring to conversation. He asks
after Zerena, forty years gone.

Nothing he says is demand,
expectations say I should know,

my job: track those left behind.

This fall, Elsie returns my letters

Jim bundled in a drawer. I study
the envelopes, addresses chronicle

places he lived, return lines mark
my move south, and later to Denmark.

I do not read the letters, I visit
the rooms where they were written.

In Grenå, the desk at the window
facing the creek and Sondre School,

I watched the sun fail its flat line
across the horizon. In the dark ache

of winter, letters were the tether.
Street numbers and cancelled stamps

are circumstantial evidence of there,
You are here stays like some bindi

marked on a gunnysack map.
I write you, you find me.

Casey Drops Blue

like an eye on a canvas tarp.
This pill bug of sky could be
a cornflower on an ice bear's back.
The petrified man has no strings attached.
For him *blue* often precedes *chair*
the way *black* aligns with *Cadillac*.
The blue chair is a lead place
where light sifts through veils,
sounds ooze like lava closing on sea.
He looks to the earth, to his green-eyed
daughter and her brown-eyed child.
He presses his feet into thick humus,
knows one drop becomes another.

On Jane's Table Everything's

for sale except the hand-blown
shot glass with her mother's
thumbprint pressed in a thin
petalled nasturtium, the way
she used her practiced ear-grip-
lift to march a son to his room.
Today it's for whiskey shots,
and the sip to seal exchanges
of objects and kept stories.
When the man offers a buck
for her father's Selah ball cap
Jane refuses. Later she gives it
to Seamus who loves the S,
she says, *This blue's from the same*
river as your eyes, he shies, touches
the brim, *no whiskey for him.*
Neighbor Margaret sets up
a wagon lined with Mason jars.
One holds an inch of tiny teeth
others cram buttons like scree.
Margaret's father died last year,
he kept the ribbons her mother
won at the fair and these jar tops
stitched with Bible verses.
The son wants her to sell her house,
he works down at the Shell.
Jane sees him days the checks
come—he parks on the lawn,
this man with the flushed face
and a mouthful of snakes.
Jane pours a shot for the guy
who buys the sweater her brother
left, extra-large ragg wool.
Here's to first snow, she toasts,

a bargain at seven dollars. As he
sips his whiskey, Jane says, *you*
now carry the heart of a lost boy,
home will be a place away, face
the wind, wear the salt spray.
He nods unsure and smiles,
looks through the jigger, its petal
like a sun where the whiskey set.

Last Night Your Mother

shows up carrying a list of titles
and magazines I have to read.
She walks me away from the table
in the Center to her home up First Hill.
She ushers me through the garden
into her place as if we had been headed
here for years. When she speaks,
her eyes listen to my face.
The first room is dark and cool,
the table white linen and wine glasses,
three cheeses, shrimp, tomato,
cilantro, blackberries, and sliced baguettes.
Beyond this still life I discover Hemingway
standing in the next room, his beard trimmed,
the white tropical shirt loose at the waist.
The curtains are pulled back, light and more light.
He never looks up. He paints watercolor.
The brush ending in his palm floats
like willow in a hint of wind.
I say nothing because she's said nothing.
He waves a mustard wash over a field,
a pencil line suggests a distant hillside.
Sit, she insists, her elegance as much ease
as taste. Her hand signs quiet
as she stops to listen to birdsong.
I carry her gesture into my day.
This is only the idea of telling you.

What Is Left

—Grenå, Denmark

When I spoke her name,
she opened and closed her eyes.
She sat front row, the first class
in a country where my ear was tin,
my bicycle black and too thin
for my frame. Putte Hembo.
I said no more—calling her name.
I heard she lived north
toward the smokestacks
where closed factories towered
like deadbeat fathers
locked behind chain link.
In dumb acres of concrete,
weeds spiked along faults
snaking yards smoke quit.
Some things never come back.
She may still live with shadows
and rust. She'd be close to forty
tonight as I recall the hiss
of wet tires, the rattle of fenders,
the click of the un-rung bell
as I rode over the tracks
crossing streets near her place.
House windows extended close
to sidewalks where I pedaled
my way to language class
expecting her to appear seated
before the evening meal.
The silent ride behind the fire
of a one-cigarette light
draws a box around a night
like a torch dismantling steel.

For Iben, Almost Forty

A breeze in the willow sweeps
new fronds over the birdhouse
with the Japanese license plate
for its tin roof. Each season
the chickadees consider and pass
its vacant eye, seeing surrenders
to sound as a slip of wind spins
again the way a song yesterday
returns Iben still eighteen, her smile
as warm as a Danish bakery.
Hedgerows line Grenå streets,
the å eases the town's length.
To speak the Danish for creek,
you open the mouth like the end
of echo, the hole in a house
with no door wedged in the center
of a tree, this place you keep for those
who might return if the right wind
plays in the hollow ache makes.

About George

Your note ends with a question
and the photo of George, his eyes
follow something off camera.
Unfair advantage knowing G dies
wearing excuses like armor fashioned
from foil. I wonder if he believed
the money he owed would keep him alive
like overdue library books or the half
tank of gas he kept in the Plymouth.
Once he showed me his favorite picture—
the Saggy Baggy Elephant's belly
rising above the surface of the pond.
He kept his Golden Book buddhas
for safety if the voices refused to stop.
When I tuned his radio to a station,
he laughed, when I left, he found
the white noise I never understood.
Some days I miss his silly fears,
the manhole covers, the crows.
Their clicking call kept him wearing
the black hat indoors, his trick
to fool them through the window.
And the hat, we dropped it
from the bridge at Van Zandt,
proper topping for his ashes drifting
the Nooksack to Bellingham Bay.

From this Window, the Widow in the Distance

—for Alice Derry

Through the red osier willow,
the flowering plum, the limbed
fir, and west, the Olympics' jagged
line marks one way to the Pacific.
In their shadow, she tends
her woodpile near Hurricane Ridge.
From this place of split and stack,
Port Angeles lies sea-before-sea,
the undammed Elwah's silt skirt
spreads a milky crescent in the bay.
Woodsmoke rises through conifer,
eases into fog. The school of the missing
is a spoon flash carom near the jetty,
a reborn river returns to the Straits,
the man who knew four cord winters
clings like pitch, sawdust, smoke in wool.

Dink's Tune

—After John Lomax's *Adventures of a Ballad Maker*

Her song sticks in my head
like a painting listing just enough
to the left to give me pause,
to lift it carefully to even,
for wind and water carried it
across the Brazos River
where the levee builders worked
Texas bottomland near College Station,
and though Dink built no walls,
she worked in water washing clothes
for her temporary man,
and as the story goes,
it was washing day not singing day,
and these songs cost a bottle of gin.
Lomax charming with juniper smoke
collects honey from a swarm of sorrow,
faretheewell, oh honey
though the faretheewell might have been
for Dink, within the year she lay buried
beneath a tree in Yazoo, Mississippi.
Dink's heavy lifting fashioned the wings
and Lomax played the keeper's part.

Finishing the Chores

—After a Rob Prout Photograph

Suppose they unraveled the neck markings
of a thousand loons and stretched them
from here to the horizon. The feather-light
miles of black ribbon and white dashes
undulate in a sea of asphalt swells rolling
south, carrying a man carrying a man's ashes.
A thousand miles, the distant call as sure
as death and Texas, this direction home.
The man carrying the man catches a stripe
of sun crossing east/west on the road ahead.
Nothing more, this road his alone with light
the only intersection between father and son
and the scattering that must be done.

Smoke and Miracles:
Meggie Asks About Marriage

—for Megan MacNichol

And what there is between a man and a woman.
And in which darkness it can best be proved.
—Eavan Boland, *Against Love Poetry*

It's Like Feeding Horses

in a snowstorm, the sky descends
like a veil and conceals pastures an acre
at a time, the order that is fence lines
disappears in the marriage of earth and sky
as the two of you dish the flakes, collars up,
heads down, and what doesn't vanish
is the idea of the horses and each other
silent within the whistling quiet of storm.
This is work whether you see it or not.

A Box of Rocks

Remember science class, the kid
with the shoebox filled with rocks,
show and tell, all that lugging and
mugging about ordinary driveway
rock, sharp-edged gravel spread
to fill potholes, clay babies in pieces
like angels with broken bottoms.
The one store-bought gem held
a crazy cave of purple glass you think
manufactured for shops at Seaside.
The kid's rocks were hand-me-down,
only the box was new, Clark's Shoes
with an attached lid that opened
and closed. Ordinary stuff without
the stories, until you saw the boy's
wide-eyed passion for what seemed
like another gray stone. In many ways,
the two of us are just a box of rocks,
pieces thrown together in the dark
some days our wishes rub together,
others, it is quiet and cold, we know
no more than the company we keep.

Breakfast

Days you wake and make
your way into the kitchen,
as if coffee were an island
you have been swimming to
for eight hours, tired, so
many strokes and those red
jellies floating in your sleep,
still this cold floor, the dogs
to put out ground you, and
what follows is breakfast
even if it's unbuttered toast
or a slice of cold pizza, this
is what comes next, and if
the job and other little bothers
interfere, there's always French
toast for dinner, or omelets.
This part of the day stays
like the dogs at the fire
like the song you hum whenever
you shop for groceries, this way
to break the fast is a lucky number,
and on those special occasions,
when you sit together without
interruptions, when afternoon
is the only thing next in the day,
this too is what it's like even
if you do not bow to it, even
though you wake to it every day.

Luck

Coincidence and chance are magic
dressed in Levi's and a T-shirt,
accident's gauzy image stumbles
like a man in heels, energy tinkles
like Sedona windchimes,
destiny is Calvin without Hobbes.
Fate strikes you as too Greek,
or Roman, it's like choosing Eros
over Cupid because cupid sounds
well, you know, picture your mother
dating online. Luck strikes home,
it's the wrong number's perfect smoke
ring around what becomes your life.

It's Like Weather

Sixty days without rain, the leaves
fall from heat, the colors fail fast
as if too soon the surrender,
loss without regret, you miss rain
like some miss breakfast, or a cigarette,
what it is—day after day sameness
until you want to scream, and you
know no one's at fault, still fault
settles it, allows blame, and blame
feels good, like a shot of vengeance,
it bruises in ways the fall colors
come alive under the skin, again
a fall, a parting, a loss you forget
with the first storm, when a fire,
tea, and a blanket find you together,
cozy enough for a change, though
too long under a relentless sky
becomes its other side, and you long
for the same sun, forgetting where
fault lay, nevertheless fault sends you
to your corners until first snow
or spring thaw turns you to each other,
and when this happens, you turn
blame to praise, overdue gratitude,
for if you made the dark, you must give
the light, if you kept the rain, you might
have brought the sun, and since no god
sleeps next to you in these beds, you share
no blame. Make praise your daily bread.

Dress Up

As kids you played school.
You sat in the desk, hands
folded while a sibling walked
the aisles, tapped a ruler
to keep your attention.
Days still start with allegiance.
Forget the hand-over-heart
pledge, it's all dress up, step
into the republic for which
you stand against another day.
This country with its strange
language, you hear *together*,
you think bailing wire or twine,
every straw is the last straw.
You have walked many times,
left bath water to turn cold,
left the bouquet on the table
for weeks until pollen's halo
circles the vase, until stems
mush in inky water. What's
left when leaving tops your
to do list, when underdog
is the only nation you know.

It's a Room

you are painting white over white.
The gouge near the light switch looks
like the place above your lip where
your sister's backswing left the sliver
of pink, took her best shot with pride
and you still standing with a handful
of blood held like a cup of cool.
No spackle for this, keep the scars
they help line up the strokes, a point
to start and cover while the marks
guide you, each nick and scrape tells
a story and a new coat is always better
when you remember the old, though
it is not about fists through a wall,
never about breaking and broken,
it's like the first snow every time, and
the little grasses stick out like bedhead
and slowly disappear in the drowsy
white you use to light this place, to keep
your quirks, the clothes left on the floor,
the way he pushes his peas to the side,
a quiet place you remake together day
after day, hour after hour, this weather.

Short Days

when morning finds you
longing for feet-in pajamas,
for hours to linger over breakfast,
coffee strong enough to chew,
you center in what's left
of the house's night sounds.
The horses steady out the window,
their shapes stay as dark dissipates,
mud room dogs rustle, the Bridgers'
ridgeline runs the waking sky.
Wind clicks the loose screen,
the rope swing is a tired clock,
the studio smells of fresh paint,
sawed wood, and it's noon.

Painting: *Bandana in Barn Window*

The boy you met is the man you kept
asking why the gray on the horse's back
turns to a cloud of stars, if shade
on the barn wall matches the cat lost
to coyotes, and would he consider
color near the shed door, say the red
of a mackinaw left after wood or
a Wellington tipped on its side. He smiles
when you ask, his shirt dappled with oils.
He points his brush handle, You, away.

What's for Dinner

no answer required, no question
mark, no apostrophe, the pronoun
says it all, what's—no ifs ands
or buts, eat your what and don't forget
to feed the dogs, they manage what
every night fresh from the sack.
Not asking, the answers settle
to the bottom—hold your breath
and open your eyes, don't ask,
this is the lost treasure.

Consider Religion

Most everybody's got one
or a version, say—jazz,
dogs, Jesus, city chickens,
organic food, list poems.
Some people have multiples,
interconnected chasms they
keep like closed mines
and we mistake caution tape
for something simple,
a swarm of yellow jackets
we think smoke will tame,
still, when you hear, Go figure,
know this is not about math.
In our neighborhood, each
new kid lost his allowance
taking the belly button bet.
Steve Bowe's brothers hauled
him out like a cash machine,
his simple scar underscored
the notion—nothing is certain.
When you ask your partner
what's wrong, and they say
Nothing, think God, belly buttons.
Think I stepped in something
sacred and this is the shaft.

Scrabble

The blank faces are one side
of every letter you need, two
are blank twice, mirror this.
Never smirk, a casual smile
hints arrogance, your words
work in conjunction with his,
except the first, star-line
double word points,
first word stands alone.
No one sees the blind draw
so defer, say Y or Z,
allow your partner first go.
Try to relax, read the signs.
If he plays *subdue* or *conquer*,
think luck of the draw,
try diplomacy look to appease
say *truce* or *kind*, the subtle turn
must look like perfect accident.
Watch for unspoken leads,
if he plays *satin*, playing *sheets*
off the S only makes sense.
Foreign words are verboten,
though if your partner plays
delicto, accept it, knowing *flagrante*
takes more letters than you'll
ever have. When tallying points,
watch for reactions, losing
is important. It must be subtle,
preferably on the final move.
If your dive is obvious, you lose
twice. Close saves face, the luck
of the draw far better than stupid.

Say "Two out of three?" without

passion, remember his best play,
remind him of it, and later,
in the heat of anger, never mention
words you could have played.

The Hands Say

A carver presses his chisel
in white pine, a ringlet coils
like chocolate, the baker crimps
the crust, one hand presses,
the other pinches dough
into flutes against slumping.
Hands know the grace of right
pressure, the practiced stroke,
the stone mason hammers
his trowel handle to break
then its blade to butter in
a half-brick at wall's end.
The left hand knows right,
seamless motion, belies
the cuts, scars, and years
of necessary failures.

Territory

Each desktop speaks
its own language,
one a jumble—a turf brick,
postcards, books, sheets
of typeface revised longhand,
one cup with coffee dregs
dried like chocolate, envelopes,
a horseshoe, correspondence.
The other, dark wood, a candle,
a miniature string of prayer flags
strung like cigarette papers.
These borders have no patrols,
everyone is the resistance,
distance winds a cursive line.

Signs

The buck explodes across the yellow
aluminum field, fore hooves rise,
hind legs drive its leap, rack and tail
point to sky. Still life moves with grace,
its warning a false lead as light streams
where rifle shot riddles true and you divine
the light shafts as fear's grand opening.
You refuse to pay homage to power,
caution works its way under the hedge.
There is no deer crossing, this is flight
and might be the lesson, a roadside
manual for daily living, these shots
failure's signature, an impotent point.
You smirk, whisper to yourself,
Stand your ground, stick to your guns.

Etch-a-Sketch

White knobs, silly way to start
on a roll you hope lasts years
or as the vows have it, till
death do us part, though film noir
does its black number with that,
and it's most often women
who take the hit, shake it off
remake the dark lines in your
favor, chicken soup for health,
rich broth and heat for two, you
pour all you have into it—
the biscuit moons buttered and
wrapped in cloth napkins, flakey
heat rising beside your spoons,
and when the image works, you
freeze it on the shelf for now.

The Math

In the first life you were
gangly, flush with freckles,
you failed to imagine a week
beyond Friday, algebra nightmares
still unfastened your head, signs
like greater than or less worked
for a game played at work—
waiting tables is greater than
lap-dancing, less than lap-dancing
with the tips, greater than
sorting apples or this black eye.
No one shared tips about jealous
husbands, boys not playing well
with others. At absolute zero
you slipped away with fifty bucks
in change, exchanged the house
you shared for Idaho, a place
like the pony you whispered over
birthday candles. A bus ticket,
your aunt's garage, following orders
Lot's wife forgot. No salt for this.
Second chances second chances
like middle school dances, boys
on one side, girls the other, acres,
endless acres of potatoes between.

Fidelity

Good name for a bank,
and your faithful dog—
whoever said *Gone to the dogs*
must have forgotten loyal,
devoted hounds free
of judgment by-your-
side sleepy-eyed love,
never stray, except
food, drink, or the curs
of heat, on second
thought, you might add
Invisible Fence
to your registry,
safer than too big
to fail, and a man
in a coffee can
under the bed takes
far too much tending.

It Ain't About Pronouns

forget he and she, his and hers,
yours works better though it's
not about ownership, you works,
this is all about a second person,
and it's plural, he and he, she and she,
we works, this is about we working
though we sometimes slip to anonymity
the indefinite somebody or no one,
anyone opens too many doors, it's not
for everyone, someone, after all,
takes a singular antecedent and Your
Antecedent calls back Better-Half,
Old Lady, Old Man, we look for words,
forwards, simplify, honor, respect
though saying it doesn't make it so.
Partner says equal, still it sounds
all business and no pleasure.
Companion is the kid they lined
next to you for YMCA fieldtrips,
Lover has passion, sounds like bragging,
Dear is smarmy, Love condescends,
Spouse rhymes with louse,
and Honey is bucket's first name.

It Might Look Like

the couple in their forty-first fall.
After weeks of raking, one maple leaf
escapes, rests within the house
where the hall turns to the bedroom.
It floats like a ruby hand on hardwood,
flared and light, untouched, for two weeks
they step around, say nothing, leave it
like a note on the mirror where a young
husband might shave or a chocolate
in foil secreted in a lunch sack,
their inattention a seasonal intention.

Anniversary

This week I carry the call like a vow,
it whispers through fir, ricochets
in cedar through alder, touches
the part burrowed where belief rests.
We mark the spot, our tell stills the trail,
we lean the way longing never makes it so.
Days later in early quiet, your owl reappears.
I hear mourning dove as clear as daybreak
at Hanne's valley near Ebeltoft.
I break the hollow bone love can be—
my problem with fidelity always fidelity.

Smoke & Miracles

You believe in the miracles
behind Smokey Robinson,
the rest is damn hard work,
like mucking stalls, ditching
irrigation water, or splitting
and stacking cordwood in July.
To choreograph endurance
imagine grace and forgiveness,
it's a twelve-step slide in honey.
Good days the train whistles
through town and you wave
safe travel, bad days you sit
at the Spar, envy those leaving,
you the tracks and your beers.

Vanish is the winner of the Wandering Aengus Book Award, and Kevin Miller's fourth poetry collection. Pleasure Boat Studio published Miller's third collection *Home & Away: The Old Town Poems* in 2009. Blue Begonia Press published *Everywhere Was Far* in 1998 and *Light That Whispers Morning*, winner of the Bumbershoot Publication Prize in 1994. He has received grants from Artist Trust, Tacoma Arts Commission, and was a member of the Jack Straw Writers Program. He was a Fulbright Teacher in Denmark and taught in the public schools of Washington State for thirty-nine years. He divides his time between Tacoma, Washington, and the Oregon high desert.

CPSIA information can be obtained
at www.ICGtesting.com
Printed in the USA
FSHW010553190121
77791FS